Chapter 1: Introduction

Butterflies are a part of Many Cultures

A butterfly is a flying insect with a small body and large, often colorful wings. Some gardeners plant specific flowers that attract butterflies. Butterflies are closely related to moths, which also have wings that are large in proportion to their bodies and antennae. There are approximately 750 species of butterflies in the United States. In comparison, there are about 17,500 species known worldwide. The Greek word for butterfly, psyche, is the same word used for soul, and this association is found across many cultures. These winged creatures have long been viewed as otherworldly messengers and heralds of good fortune and joy. Butterflies have inspired humans for

millennia with their delicate nature and the belief of the mythical power they possess. Native Americans considered butterflies as almost magical creatures, they were viewed as symbols of hope, a new beginning or a rebirth of sorts. They often decorate their clothes, teepees, and possessions with butter☐ies. as a way to honor the butterfly.

In Chinese culture, butterflies are symbols of freedom, love, earthly beauty, and can represent the human soul of a loved ones who have pasted. A pair of butterflies fluttering together is seen as a symbol of undying love. In some other cultures, particularly in Asia, butterflies are often associated with long life, and good luck. Yellow butterflies can symbolize a positive future and a sign of good fortunes. Seeing

one might mean good news or positive changes are headed your way, good health or long life maybe in store. Spiritually, a yellow butterfly can symbolize that you're near a spiritual awakening. It

The Wonders of the Monarch Butterfly

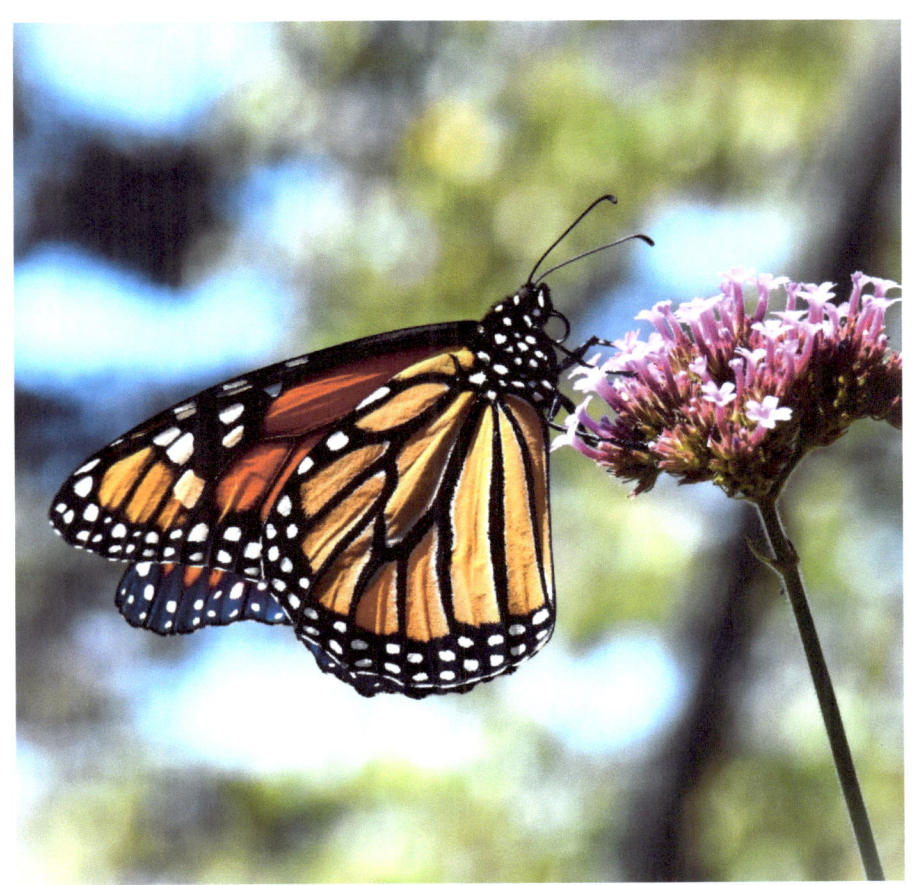

Table Of Contents

Chapter 1: Introduction 2
Chapter 2: Monarch Life Cycle 2
Chapter 3: Monarch Spotlight 2
Chapter 4: Migration Patterns...2
Chapter 5: Conservation 2
Chapter 6: Monarch Garden 2
Chapter 7: Photo Techniques..2
Chapter 8: Conclusion 2
The Wonders of the Monarch Butterfly 1

might also be a sign that your passed loved ones are thinking of you or even their spirt is near you.

From representing the human soul in Greek philosophy to symbolizing joy, happiness, and exhilaration in French folklore, butterflies have woven their way through European culture, art, and history. Their carefree nature is often connected with the fleeting essence of happiness and the enrichment of one's soul. Over the years butterflies have become a source of great comfort for both the mind and the sprit, being a symbol of care free living and freedom.

In Japanese culture, butterflies carry a number of meanings but are most closely associated with the symbolism of transformation. They are closely linked with recently departed spirits and, consequently, are represented in a number of traditional family crests. While the elder members of the Japanese family are honored for the wisdom that comes with living a long life, the butterfly is respected as a spirit of a departed family member.

In many African cultures, butterflies symbolize transformation or a spiritual rebirth. Their life cycle, from caterpillar to chrysalis to butterfly, mirrors the journey of personal growth and development, resonating deeply with themes of resilience and renewal. The butterfly's ability to fly freely symbolizes freedom from earthly

Constraints and the pursuit of higher spiritual truths. Butterflies can also represent positive change in appearance, the tenderness of African souls, and the essence of life.

In Korean culture, there are many symbols of transformation and the cycle of life. In Korea, the butterfly symbolizes prosperity and contentment. They are generally associated with light and beauty, but they also have a dark side—one filled with ugliness and contradiction. The interpretation depends on the circumstances of the encounter. The monarch butterfly, in particular, has been a popular subject included in various art forms, such as paintings and porcelain works.

In Christianity, the butterfly has long been a symbol of the resurrection, for it disappears.

Into a cocoon, it appears dead, but later emerges far more beautiful and powerful than before. The three stages of the butterfly's metamorphosis are symbolic of the three stages in the life cycle of Jesus Christ and the Christian journey: spiritual transformation, awakening, and hope. Some people also see these beautiful creatures as messengers from the angelic realm. If you're going through a tough time and butterflies appear around you, take it as a sign that angels are watching over you and helping you along the way.

Adult monarch butterflies possess two pairs of brilliant orange-red wings, featuring black veins and white spots along the edges. Males, who possess distinguishing black dots along the veins of their wings, are slightly bigger than females.

Monarchs are large, beautifully colored butterflies that are easy to recognize by their striking orange, black, and white markings. Monarchs are large, beautifully colored butterflies that are easy to recognize by their striking orange, black, and white markings.

During the following pages we will be exploring the wonders of one of the most Beautiful and sought-after butterflies that ever grace the gentle summer winds, the monarch butterfly. Through these words and photographs, we hope to increase appreciation for this wondrous creature while preserving it for future generations.

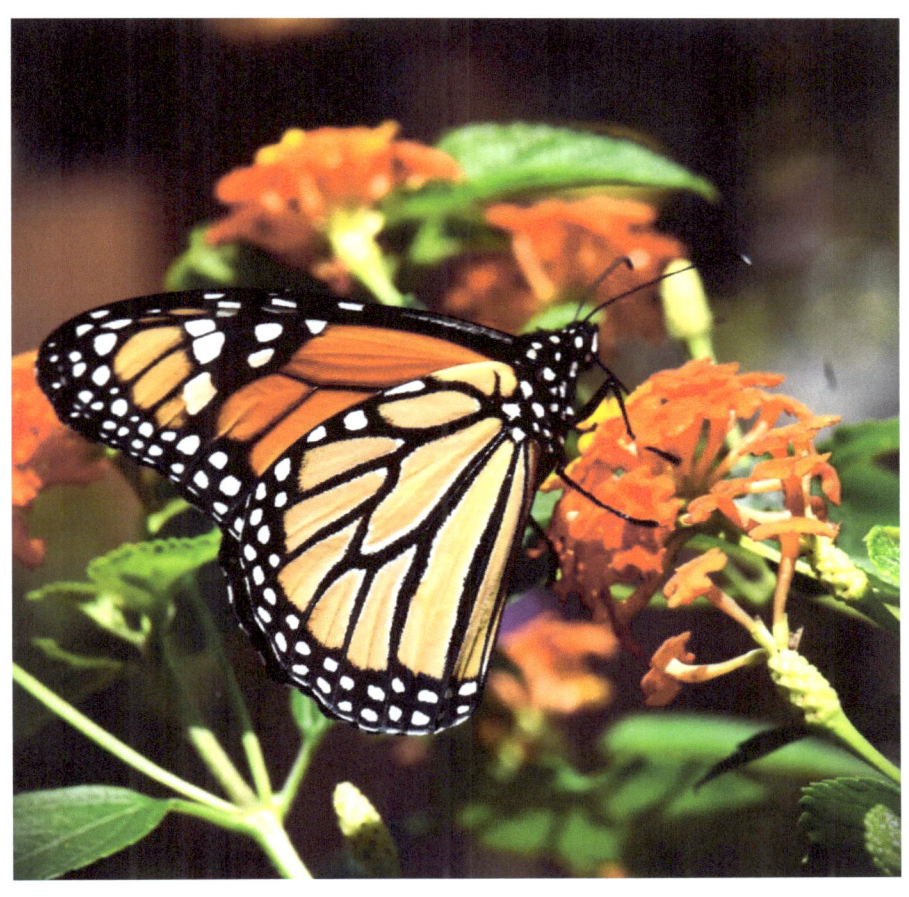

Chapter 2: Monarch Life Cycle

Stages of Development: Egg to Adult

The life cycle of the monarch butterfly is a fascinating process that unfolds in distinct stages, each contributing to the majestic transformation from egg to adult. Understanding these stages is essential for photographers looking to capture the beauty of monarchs in their various forms. The journey begins when a female monarch lays her eggs, typically on the underside of milkweed leaves, which serve as the first food source for the emerging caterpillars. The eggs are tiny, about the size of a pinhead, and are often laid in clusters, making them a compelling subject for close-up photography. Capturing these eggs in their natural habitat not only highlights the reproductive process.

but also highlights the importance of milkweed in monarch conservation efforts.

Once the eggs hatch, the next stage begins: the larval or caterpillar phase. Monarch caterpillars are easily recognizable by their striking black, yellow, and white stripes. This stage is critical for growth, as the caterpillar consumes vast amounts of milkweed to store energy for its transformation. Photographers can take advantage of this phase by experimenting with macro photography techniques to showcase the intricate details of the caterpillar's anatomy and its interactions with the milkweed plant. Observing this stage also offers insights into the caterpillar's defense mechanisms, including its ability to absorb toxic compounds from milkweed, which make it unpalatable to predators.

The caterpillar eventually enters the pupal stage, forming a chrysalis that is often a stunning emerald green, adorned with gold accents.

This transformation is one of the most photogenic moments in the monarch's life cycle. The chrysalis, which hangs from a secure surface, can be photographed to emphasize the delicate balance between fragility and resilience. It is also a critical period during which the caterpillar undergoes metamorphosis, a process that can take several days. Photographers can capture the tension of this transformation by documenting the changes in light and color as the chrysalis matures, culminating in the emergence of the adult butterfly.

The final stage is the emergence of the adult monarch butterfly, a moment that symbolizes both completion and renewal. As the wings unfurl and drying, they reveal the vibrant colors and patterns that make monarchs so recognizable. This moment is fleeting, emphasizing the need for photographers to be prepared to capture the excitement and beauty of the newly emerged butterfly. The adult monarch will soon embark on its migration journey, a critical aspect of its life cycle that showcases the butterfly's resilience and adaptability. Documenting this stage not only highlights the beauty of the butterflies but also serves as a reminder of their incredible migration patterns, which span thousands of miles.

Lastly, understanding the lifecycle of monarch butterflies can enhance the storytelling aspect of photography. The entire migration journey is part of a much larger cycle that includes breeding.

caterpillar development, and eventual pupation. By aligning their photography with the life cycle stages of the monarchs, photographers can create a compelling visual narrative that not only showcases the migration itself but also educates audiences about the importance of protecting these butterflies throughout their entire life cycle. This holistic approach enhances the aesthetic appeal of the photographs and emphasizes the interconnectedness of monarchs with their ecosystems, fostering a deeper appreciation for these wondrous creatures.

In conclusion, understanding the stages of development from egg to adult is vital for photographers focused on monarch butterflies. Each stage presents unique

opportunities to capture the essence of these incredible creatures while shedding light on the broader themes of conservation and ecosystem impact.

By documenting the entire life cycle, photographers can contribute to the storytelling of monarchs, raising awareness of the challenges they face and the importance of preserving their habitats. This comprehensive approach not only enhances photographic portfolios but also fosters a deeper appreciation for the wonders of nature and the vital role butterflies play in our ecosystems.

Through the chrysalis, the day before the adult emerges, you can see the orange and black wings of the Monarch butterfly inside.

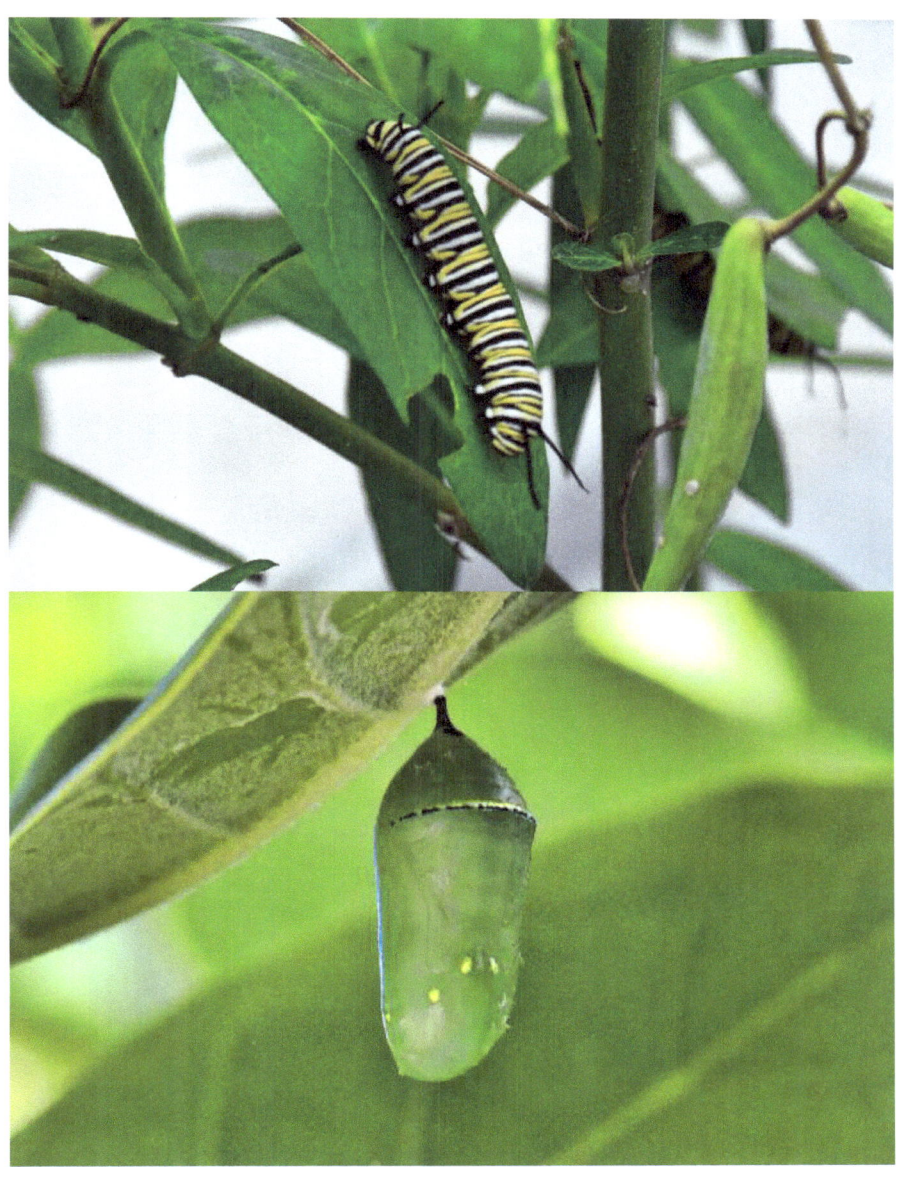

Chapter 3: Monarch Spotlight

The Importance of Monarch Butterflies

The monarch butterfly, with its striking orange and black wings, represents not only beauty but also the intricate connections within ecosystems. This iconic species plays a crucial role in pollination, which is vital for the reproduction of many flowering plants. As photographers, capturing the essence of monarchs in their natural habitats allows for a deeper appreciation of their ecological importance. The presence of these butterflies often indicates a healthy environment, making them a key indicator species for assessing ecosystem health.

Monarch butterflies are renowned for their remarkable migration patterns, traveling

thousands of miles from North America to central Mexico. This annual journey is not just a spectacle for wildlife photographers; it serves ecological functions that go beyond mere aesthetics. During their migration, monarchs facilitate the pollination of various plants across vast landscapes, thereby contributing to biodiversity.

Understanding these migration routes can be invaluable for photographers seeking to document the life stages and behaviors of these butterflies in different geographical contexts.

Conservation efforts for monarch butterflies have gained momentum in recent years, highlighting their declining populations due to habitat loss, pesticide use, and climate change. Photographers have a unique opportunity to raise awareness about these threats through their work. By documenting conservation initiatives, such as the planting of milkweed and native flowers, photographers can illustrate the importance of preserving habitats that support monarchs. This visual storytelling can inspire viewers to engage in local conservation efforts, fostering a collective responsibility toward protecting these vital pollinators.

Gardening for monarch butterflies is another avenue where photographers can make an impact. Creating habitats that provide food and shelter for these butterflies not only benefits the species but also enriches the photographer's opportunities for capturing stunning images. By incorporating native plants into gardens,

Photographers can attract monarchs and document their life cycles, from egg to caterpillar to chrysalis and finally to adult butterfly. These interactions offer a unique lens through which to explore the intricate life cycle of monarchs, underscoring the importance of nurturing environments that sustain them.

The migration patterns of monarch butterflies further illustrate their significance in ecosystem dynamics. Each year, they embark on a remarkable journey spanning thousands of miles, navigating through varying climates and landscapes. This migration is not only a spectacle to behold but also a complex phenomenon that impacts numerous ecosystems along their route. As photographers, capturing the essence of these migrations can help convey.

The urgency of conservation efforts. By documenting the various stages of their journey, you can highlight the critical habitats that must be preserved to ensure the survival of this iconic species.

In summary, the impact of monarch butterflies on ecosystems is profound and deserving of attention. As photographers, your ability to document their beauty and ecological significance can play a pivotal role in raising awareness about the importance of monarch conservation. By focusing on their role as pollinators, their dependence on native plants, and the intricacies of their migration patterns, you can create compelling narratives that inspire action and foster a deeper appreciation for these remarkable insects. Through your lens, the wonders of the monarch butterfly can serve.

as a catalyst for environmental stewardship and a celebration of the interconnectedness of life.

The monarch butterfly, often referred to as the monarch, belongs to the milkweed butterfly family Nymphalidae. While these butterflies are originally from North and South America, they have also expanded to other warm regions where milkweed is found.

Monarch butterflies embark on a marvelous migratory phenomenon. They travel between 1,200 and 2,800 miles or more from the northeast United States, and southeast Canada to the mountain forests in central Mexico, where they find the right climate conditions to hibernate from the beginning of November to mid-March.

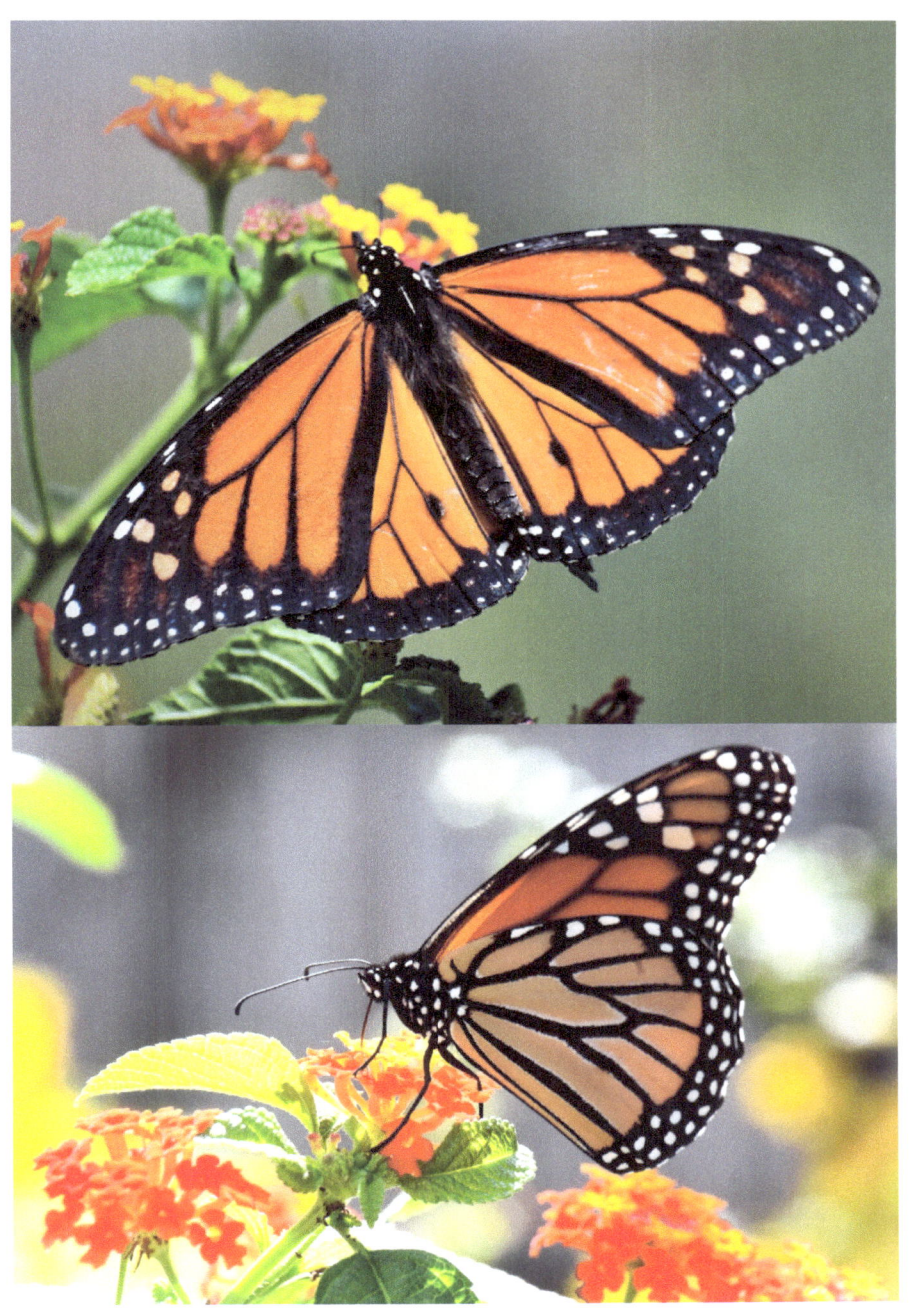

Chapter 4: Migration Patterns

The Great Migration: A Journey Like No Other

The great migration of monarch butterflies is one of the most remarkable natural phenomena on our planet, a journey that spans thousands of miles and captivates the hearts and lenses of photographers worldwide. Each year, millions of these delicate insects embark on a migration from their breeding grounds in North America to the warm, sheltered forests of central Mexico. This epic journey, often covering up to 3,000 miles, showcases not only the resilience and instinctual navigation skills of these butterflies but also highlights the vital role they play in our ecosystems. For photographers, capturing the essence of this

migration offers a unique opportunity to document the beauty and fragility of life in motion.

Understanding the migration patterns of monarch butterflies is crucial for photographers aiming to capture their journey. Monarchs typically begin their migration in late summer and early fall, as daylight decreases and temperatures drop. They instinctively follow a route that leads them to specific overwintering sites in Mexico, where they cluster in large numbers on Oyamel Fir trees. Knowing when and where to position oneself to photograph these magnificent creatures requires an understanding of their life cycle and behavior. Photographers can enhance their chances of capturing stunning images by researching migration timelines and.

identifying key stopover sites along the route.

Conservation efforts play a significant role in ensuring the survival of the monarch migration, and photographers can contribute by raising awareness through their work. The decline in monarch populations due to habitat loss, climate change, and pesticide use poses a serious threat to this epic journey. By documenting the beauty of these butterflies and the challenges they face, photographers can help promote conservation initiatives aimed at protecting their habitats. Collaborating with local conservation organizations or participating in citizen science projects can provide photographers with valuable insights while also allowing them to give back to the environment through their art.

Additionally, the availability of food sources plays a critical role in determining migration. Human activity, particularly land use changes, also significantly impacts migration routes. Urban development, agricultural practices, and habitat destruction can create barriers to migration or lead to the loss of critical stopover sites. Photographers documenting these changes can highlight the urgent need for conservation measures. By showcasing the stark contrast between healthy habitats and those affected by human encroachment, photographers can raise awareness about the importance of preserving migratory pathways for monarch butterflies and the ecosystems they inhabit..

Biological factors, including the inherent migratory instincts of butterflies and their dependence on specific environmental

 signals, significantly influence their migration routes. Monarchs utilize a mix of the Earth's magnetic field, the sun's position, and olfactory signals from their surroundings to navigate. Gaining insight into these biological processes helps photographers identify optimal times and locations for photographing migration events. Capturing monarchs during these pivotal moments can result in stunning images that not only highlight their beauty but also emphasize their extraordinary journey and the challenges they encounter.

To sum up, the migration routes of monarch butterflies are influenced by various environmental, biological, and human factors. For photographers, understanding these elements is crucial not only for taking breathtaking photos but

also for supporting conservation initiatives. By tailoring their work to the needs of these remarkable insects, photographers can significantly contribute to increasing awareness about monarch migration, advocating for habitat conservation, and highlighting the interconnectedness of life within ecosystems.

The emergence of the adult monarch is a pivotal moment that signifies the end of its life cycle. As these butterflies unfurl their wings for the first time, they begin a journey that can span thousands of miles during migration. This stage is crucial not just for the individual butterfly but for the species as a whole, as it significantly impacts pollination and the health of ecosystems. Photographershave the opportunity to capture the awe-inspiring moment of

emergence and the subsequent flight illustrate the resilience and beauty of the monarch butterfly. By documenting these key life cycle events, photographers not only create stunning visuals but also contribute to a deeper understanding of the challenges faced by monarchs and the importance of protecting their migratory routes and breeding grounds.

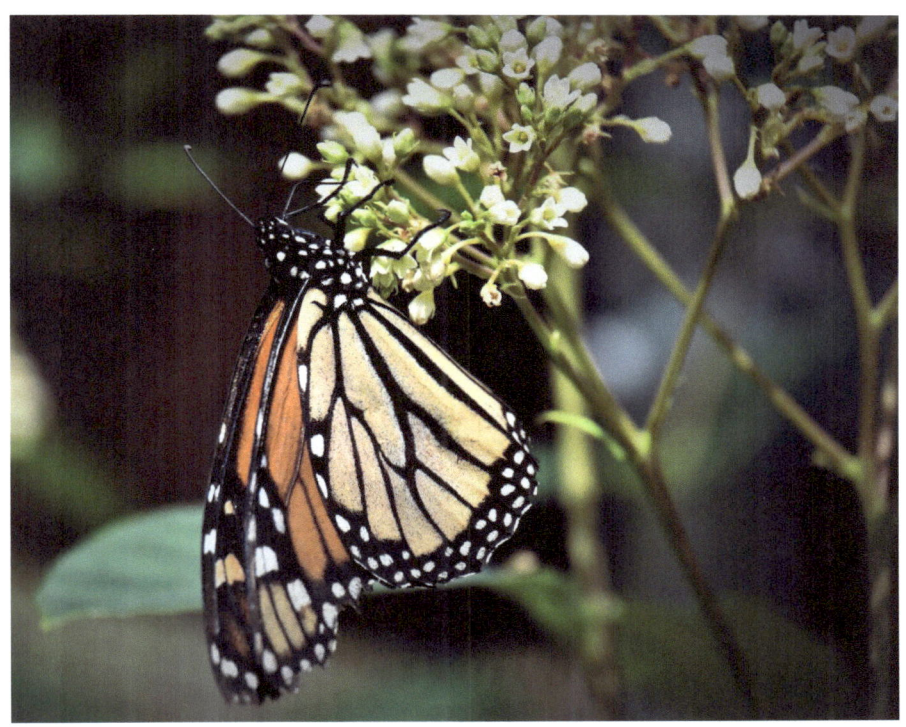

Environmental Factors on Development

Environmental factors play a crucial role in the development of monarch butterflies, affecting their life cycle, migration patterns, and overall population health. Understanding these factors is essential for photographers aiming to capture the beauty of these remarkable insects. Various environmental factors, such as climate, habitat availability, and food sources, contribute to the monarch's life cycle and migration routes, providing photographers with unique opportunities to document their behaviors and interactions within the ecosystem.

Climate change has emerged as one of the most significant environmental factors impacting monarch butterflies. Fluctuations in temperature and weather patterns can disrupt migration schedules, lead to habitat loss, and affect the availability of milkweed— the primary food source for monarch caterpillars.

Photographers can observe and document how these changes manifest in the butterflies' behavior, such as altered migration timings or changes in breeding grounds. Capturing these moments provides valuable insights into the ongoing challenges monarchs face in a rapidly changing world.

Habitat availability is another critical factors in the development of monarch butterflies. Urbanization, agricultural expansion, and deforestation have led to the degradation of natural habitats essential for their survival. Photographers can play a vital role in conservation efforts by documenting the

impact of these environmental changes on monarch populations. By focusing on areas where milkweed and nectar-producing plants thrive, photographers can highlight conservation initiatives and showcase the importance of preserving these ecosystems for the health of monarchs and other pollinators.

Life Cycle Events and Their Significance

The life cycle of the monarch butterfly is a remarkable journey, encompassing a series of key events that are crucial for its survival and reproduction. Understanding these stages—egg, larva (caterpillar), pupa (chrysalis), and adult butterfly—provides photographers with the opportunity to capture the beauty and complexity of these insects. Each phase not only represents a significant transformation in the

monarch's life but also highlights the delicate balance of ecosystems in which they thrive. By documenting these stages, photographers contribute to a greater awareness of the species and the conservation efforts that aim to protect them.

The first stage of the monarch's life begins when a female butterfly lays eggs on the underside of milkweed leaves, the only plant that monarch larvae can consume. This event is significant not only for the continuation of the species but also for the health of milkweed populations. Photographers capturing this moment can emphasize the intricate relationship between the monarch and its host plant, showcasing the role of milkweed as a vital component.   the ecosystem. Highlighting these eggs

 the ecosystem. Highlighting these eggs through macro photography not only brings attention to their delicate nature but also serves to educate viewers about the importance of preserving milkweed habitats.

As the eggs hatch, the larvae emerge and enter their caterpillar stage, a phase characterized by rapid growth and voracious feeding. This stage is crucial for the caterpillars as they must consume enough milkweed to store energy for metamorphosis. Photographers have a unique opportunity to document the caterpillar's transformation and feeding behaviors, which can be vibrant and visually stunning. Capturing images of the caterpillars amidst lush green leaves or in various stages of growth can illustrate their importance in the broader ecological picture,

as they contribute to the nutrient cycle within their habitats.

After several weeks of feeding and growing, caterpillars enter the pupal stage, forming a chrysalis. This transformation is one of the most awe-inspiring events in the monarch's life cycle. During this time, the caterpillar undergoes a complete metamorphosis, and the changes that occur within the chrysalis are remarkable. Photographers can focus on this stage to convey the sense of anticipation and mystery that surrounds the metamorphosis process. Images of chrysalises hanging from branches can evoke a sense of wonder and highlight the vulnerability of this life stage, underscoring the need for conservation efforts to protect these habitats from environmental threats.

In conclusion, the importance of monarch butterflies transcends their aesthetic appeal. These remarkable insects are critical players in ecosystems, and photographers hold the power to spotlight their significance. Through thoughtful documentation of their migration, conservation efforts, and gardening practices, photographers can contribute to a broader understanding of monarchs while inspiring action to protect them. As stewards of the natural world, photographers can use their art to advocate for the survival of monarch butterflies, ensuring that future generations can marvel at their beauty and the wonders they bring to our ecosystems.

Overview of Ecosystem Impact

The ecosystem impact of Monarch butterflies is profound and multifaceted,

and intertwining with ecological dynamics, biodiversity, and the health of the environments they inhabit. As photographers, understanding this impact not only enriches your appreciation of these magnificent creatures but also deepens your commitment to capturing their beauty in a way that reflects their vital role in our ecosystems. Monarchs serve as indicators of ecosystem health, and their presence often signifies a balanced and thriving environment. Their migratory patterns, for instance, demonstrate the interconnectedness of habitats across vast distances, emphasizing the necessity for conservation efforts that protect not just the butterflies, but the entire ecosystems they rely on.

Timing and Duration of Migration

Gardening for monarch butterflies is another essential aspect of supporting their migration. Creating butterfly-friendly gardens filled with native nectar plants and host plants for caterpillars can significantly impact local populations. Photographers can use their platforms to educate others about the importance of these gardens, showcasing not only photographs of adult monarchs feeding on flowers but also the intricate details of their life cycle as they transform from caterpillars to butterflies. Highlighting these interactions in their work not only enriches their portfolio but also serves a greater purpose in promoting biodiversity and ecosystem health.

The Great Migration of monarch butterflies

represents a journey that beautifully intertwines art, science, and conservation. For photographers, it offers a unique chance to narrate a story that transcends simple visuals. By gaining insight into migration patterns, supporting conservation initiatives, promoting butterfly-friendly gardening, and documenting the monarchs' life cycle, photographers can craft meaningful narratives that connect with audiences. This journey, characterized by the gentle flutter of wings and the resilience of nature, invites photographers to observe, capture, and share the wonders of the natural world.

The timing and duration of monarch migration are critical factors that photographers must consider when planning their shoots. Each fall, millions of monarchs embark on an epic journey from their

summer breeding grounds in North America to their wintering sites in central Mexico. This migration, which can cover thousands of miles, typically begins in late August and continues through

October. Understanding this timeline is essential for capturing the stunning moments of their departure and the breathtaking landscapes they traverse. Photographers need to be aware of the specific windows when Monarchs are most active, allowing them to optimize their chances of documenting this natural spectacle.

As monarchs migrate, they follow a special route that is affected by environmental factors such as temperature, wind patterns, and food availability. The journey is not a straight line; instead, it involves multiple

stopovers. where the butterflies rest and refuel on nectar-rich flowers. This presents an opportunity to observe and capture the butterflies in various habitats along their migration path. Identifying key locations where monarchs are known to congregate, such as gardens, parks, and natural reserves can enhance the chances of obtaining compelling images that showcase both the butterflies and their transient environments.

Monarch butterflies also have a unique relationship with the plants they depend on, particularly milkweed. This plant is not just a food source for the caterpillars; it is an integral part of the monarch's life cycle and a critical component of the ecosystem. By choosing to photograph monarchs in their native habitats, you can draw attention to the importance of protecting milkweed and

other native plants that support not only monarchs but a myriad of other species. Your images can inspire gardeners and conservationists alike to cultivate these plants, fostering a healthier ecosystem for all.

Duration is another variable to consider in monarch photography. The migration process can take several weeks, with some individuals arriving at their wintering grounds as late as mid-November. This extended timeframe allows photographers to track the monarchs over the course of their journey, observing changes in behavior, coloration, and even the impact of weather conditions on their migration. By documenting different stages of the migration, photographers can tell a more comprehensive story about these

remarkable insects, providing insights into their resilience and adaptability.

The timing and duration of migration also have implications for Monarch butterfly conservation efforts. As climate change alters weather patterns, the timing of these migrations may shift, potentially hindering the Monarchs' survival rates.
Photographers play a vital role in raising awareness about these changes by capturing and sharing their experiences. By highlighting the beauty and challenges of Monarch migration through their lenses, photographers can contribute to conservation narratives, inspiring action to protect critical habitats and migration routes.

Food sources, particularly the availability of milkweed and nectar-rich flowers, directly

effect the growth and development of monarch butterflies. The presence of diverse plants not only provides essential nutrition for adult butterflies but also creates suitable breeding grounds for eggs and caterpillars. Photographers can capture the delicate relationship between monarchs and their preferred plants, illustrating the interconnectedness of species within their habitats. By focusing on gardens and conservation areas that support monarch populations, photographers can advocate for gardening practices that promote biodiversity and enhance local ecosystems.

Monarch butterflies play an important role in ecosystems by serving as pollinators. While they are not as efficient as bees, they help with the reproduction of numerous flowering plants.

The migration patterns of monarchs are influenced by a variety of environmental factors, including weather and geographic obstacles. These long-distance travelers depend on specific cues for navigation, presenting photographers with the chance to capture their extraordinary migrations. By understanding the environmental factors involved, photographers can better predict the optimal times and locations for photographing monarchs in flight. This not only enhances their portfolios but also raises awareness about the challenges these butterflies encounter, highlighting the importance of conservation and sustainable practices to secure their future survival.

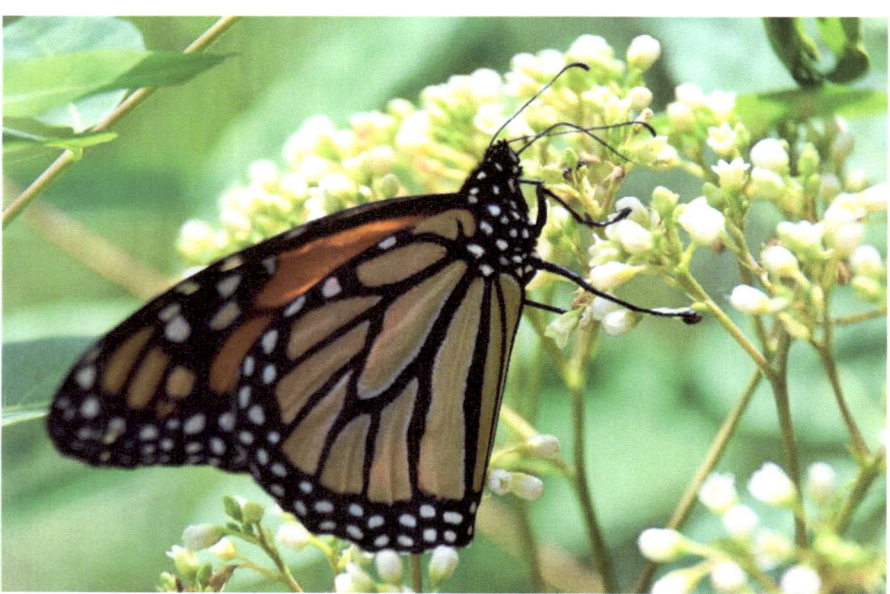

Chapter 5: Conservation

Current Threats to Monarch Populations

The majestic monarch butterfly, known for its vibrant orange and black wings, is facing a myriad of threats that jeopardize its population and migratory patterns. As photographers dedicated to capturing the beauty of these insects, understanding the current challenges they encounter is essential not only for your work but also for the conservation of this iconic species. These challenges are not only ecological but also deeply intertwined with human activities that have disrupted the delicate balance of their habitats.

Pesticide use is an additional threat that continues to impact monarch populations.

The application of neonicotinoids and other harmful chemicals in agriculture not only affects insects directly but also reduces food sources and habitat quality. This can have a cascading effect on the entire ecosystem, impacting not only monarchs but also other pollinators. Photographers have a unique opportunity to document this relationship. between pesticide use and declining monarch populations, providing a visual narrative that underscores the need for policy changes and sustainable practices.

The growing presence of invasive species presents a serious threat to the native flora that monarchs rely on. These invasive plants can overwhelm milkweed, resulting in fewer breeding sites for the butterflies. As photographers, capturing the fragile balance of ecosystems that support monarchs can

highlight the interconnectedness of various species. By featuring the beauty of native plants and their importance in sustaining monarch populations, you can help promote a greater awareness of the necessity for ecological preservation.

One of the most pressing threats to monarch populations is habitat loss, primarily due to agricultural expansion and urban development. The conversion of natural landscapes into monoculture farming and urban sprawl has led to the destruction of milkweed, the sole host plant for monarch caterpillars. Without sufficient milkweed, monarchs cannot reproduce, which directly impacts their life cycle and migratory success. The monarch populations are currently threatened by habitat loss, climate change, pesticide application, and invasive

species. Each of these issues poses significant challenges that demand urgent action from both conservationists and the general public. As photographers, your talent for capturing the beauty of these butterflies and their habitats can be instrumental in fostering awareness and promoting their conservation. By sharing your vision, you can motivate others to participate in the initiatives that will help ensure that future generations can still appreciate the marvels of monarch butterflies.

Factors Contributing to Migration Routes

Migration routes of monarch butterflies are influenced by a complex interplay of environmental, biological, and anthropogenic factors. Understanding these factors is crucial for photographers aiming to capture the beauty of these insects in their

in their natural habitats. Understanding the factors that influence migration patterns allows photographers to improve their work and support conservation initiatives. Lets examines the key elements that drive monarch butterfly migration and their significance for photography and conservation.

One of the most important factors in migration routes is climate. monarchs are highly sensitive to temperature changes, which dictate their movement across North America. As they travel from their summer breeding grounds in the United States and Canada to their wintering sites in Mexico, changes in weather patterns can alter their paths. Photographers should be aware of seasonal climate changes and how they may affect the timing and location of the

migration. Allowing them to capturing images of monarchs with unique opportunities in unexpected locations.

Grassroots Conservation Initiatives

Grassroots and global conservation initiatives play a crucial role in the preservation of monarch butterflies, whose populations have been declining due to habitat loss, climate change, and pesticide use. These efforts are increasingly important for photographers who seek to capture the beauty of these remarkable insects while contributing to their survival. Understanding the interplay between local actions and worldwide movements can inspire photographers to engage with conservation efforts, amplifying their impact through their art.

At the grassroots level, community-based conservation projects are essential for supporting monarch habitats. Local gardening initiatives that encourage the planting of milkweed and nectar plants create vital environments for monarchs at various stages of their life cycle. Photographers can participate by documenting these efforts, showcasing not only the butterflies but also the communities that nurture their habitats. By highlighting the relationship between local gardens and monarch populations, photographers can raise awareness about the importance of native plants and inspire others to create their own butterfly-friendly spaces.

Global conservation initiatives, such as the Monarch Joint Venture and the North American Monarch Conservation Plan, aim

 to unite efforts across borders to protect migratory routes and breeding grounds.

These organizations focus on research, habitat restoration, and public education. Photographers can play a significant role by capturing the stories of these initiatives, from fieldwork to community engagement. Through compelling imagery, they can illustrate the interconnectedness of ecosystems and the importance of international cooperation in safeguarding monarchs for future generations.

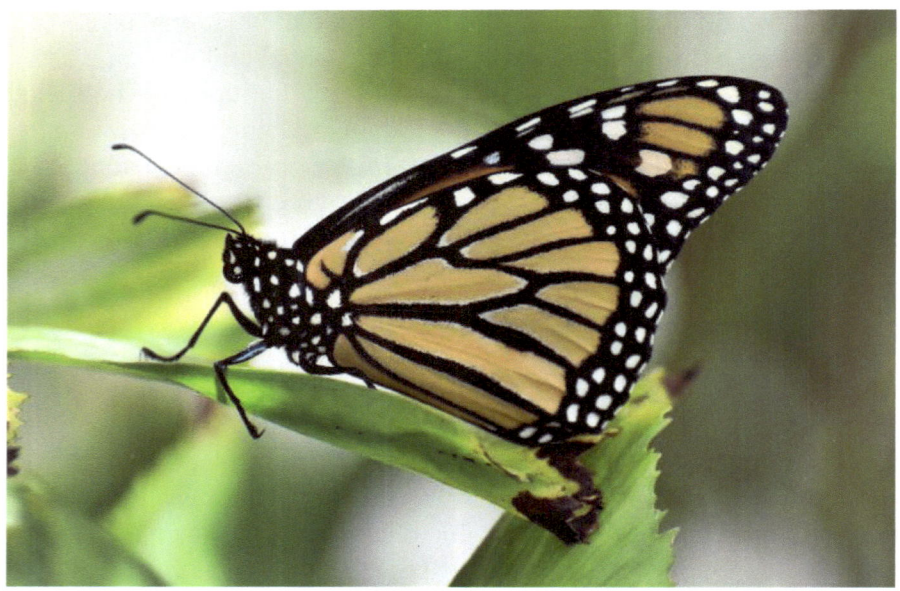

In addition to documenting conservation efforts, photographers can also engage directly with local communities by leading workshops that educate participants about monarch butterfly migration patterns and their ecological significance. These workshops can teach participants how to create habitats conducive to the butterflies' life cycles, providing them with the knowledge and tools to contribute to conservation. By fostering a deeper understanding of monarchs, photographers not only enrich their own work but also empower others to appreciate and protect these delicate creatures.

Ultimately, the synergy between grassroots actions and global initiatives fosters a comprehensive approach to conservation that benefits both monarch butterflies and

the ecosystems they inhabit. Photographers, as storytellers and educators, have a unique opportunity to shine a light on these efforts. By documenting the beauty of monarchs and the vital work being done to protect them, photographers can inspire others to take action, ensuring that future generations can continue to marvel at the wings and wonders of monarch butterflies.

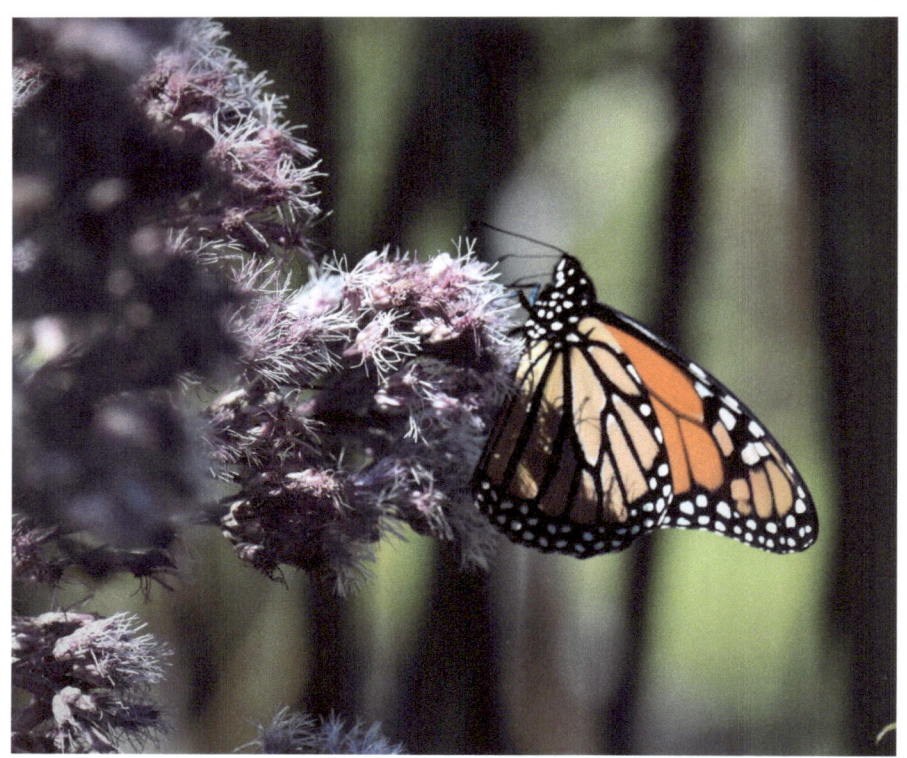

How Photographers Can Contribute to Conservation

Photographers possess a unique ability to aid conservation efforts through their art and storytelling. In the context of monarch butterflies, these visual storytellers can play a pivotal role in raising awareness about the challenges facing these iconic insects. By capturing the beauty of monarchs in their natural habitats, photographers can inspire viewers to appreciate the delicate balance of ecosystems and the need for conservation initiatives. Through their lens, photographers not only document the life cycle and migration patterns of monarch butterflies but also highlight the critical role these creatures play in our environment.

One significant way photographers can contribute to conservation is by creating compelling imagery that showcases the monarch butterfly's journey. By documenting the awe-inspiring migration from North America to central Mexico, photographers can provide insight into the threats these butterflies face, such as habitat loss and climate change. High-quality images can serve as powerful tools in advocacy campaigns, encouraging individuals and organizations to support conservation efforts.

By sharing their photographs through exhibitions, publications, and social media, photographers can reach a broader audience, fostering a deeper understanding of the importance of preserving monarch habitats.

In addition to raising awareness, photographers can actively participate in gardening initiatives that support monarch

butterfly populations. By promoting the establishment of butterfly gardens filled with native milkweed and nectar plants, photographers can demonstrate how individual actions contribute to larger conservation goals. This not only enriches their photography subjects but also creates a tangible impact on local ecosystems. Workshops or guided photo walks that emphasize gardening for monarchs can engage communities and empower them to take part in conservation efforts while honing their photography skills.

Moreover, photographers can collaborate with conservation organizations to document ongoing research and restoration projects. By providing visual documentation, they can help raise funds and support for these initiatives. Photographers can create promotional materials, including stunning visuals for brochures and websites, that highlight the work being done to protect monarch habitats. This partnership can amplify the message of conservation groups and encourage more people to get involved, whether through volunteer work, donations, or advocacy.

Finally, photographers have the opportunity to educate the public about the life cycle and behaviors of monarch butterflies through their work. By capturing each stage of the monarch's development—from egg to caterpillar to chrysalis and finally to adult—their images can serve as educational tools in both formal and informal settings. Photographers can develop multimedia presentations or educational social media campaigns that not only showcase their

artistry but also impart valuable knowledge about monarchs and their ecological significance.Through these efforts, photographers can cultivate a sense of stewardship among their audience, motivating them to engage in practices that support the survival of these remarkable butterflies.

Chapter 6: Monarch Garden

Creating a Monarch-Friendly Garden

Creating a monarch-friendly garden is an essential step for photographers looking to capture the beauty of these iconic butterflies while contributing to their conservation. Monarch butterflies rely heavily on specific plants for feeding and breeding, making the garden environment a critical factor in their survival. By understanding the needs of these butterflies and selecting the right plants, photographers can create a vibrant habitat that not only attracts monarchs but also provides stunning backdrops for photography.

To begin, it is crucial to incorporate milkweed species, which are the primary

host plants for monarch caterpillars. Milkweed provides the necessary nutrients for caterpillars to thrive and undergo their metamorphosis. Selecting local varieties of milkweed, such as common milkweed (Asclepias syriaca) or swamp milkweed (Asclepias incarnata), can increase the likelihood of attracting monarchs, as these plants are better suited to the local climate and soil conditions. Additionally, incorporating a diverse range of common plants can further enhance the habitat. nectar-producing plants, such as asters, cone□owers, and zinnias, will provide a continuous food source for adult butter□ies throughout the growing season.

Creating a suitable habitat also involves considering the layout and maintenance of the garden. Photographers should aim for a sunny spot with minimal disturbance, as monarchs are attracted to warm areas where they can bask. Grouping plants in clusters rather than scattering them will help create a visually appealing landscape while attracting more butterflies. It is important to minimize the use of pesticides or harmful chemicals, as these can deter monarchs and other beneficial insects. Regular watering and weeding will help maintain the garden's health, ensuring that it remains inviting for both monarchs and photographers.

In addition to plant selection and garden maintenance, providing shelter and resources is vital for creating a monarch-friendly environment. Incorporating native shrubs or trees can offer refuge for butterflies during inclement weather and a place for them to roost. Additionally,

including shallow water sources, such as birdbaths or small ponds, can help fulfill their hydration needs. Photographers may find that these varied elements provide unique photographic opportunities, capturing the beauty of butterflies interacting with their environment in dynamic ways.

Participating in community initiatives can enhance the effects of individual gardens. By joining local conservation projects or working alongside other gardeners, photographers can support wider efforts to restore monarch populations. Exchanging experiences and advice on establishing successful monarch gardens can strengthen the community among butterfly lovers. As photographers document the beauty of monarchs in their gardens, they significantly

As photographers document the beauty of monarchs in their gardens, they significantly contribute to raising awareness about the need for conservation, ensuring that future generations will appreciate the splendor of these remarkable creatures.

Essential Plants for Monarch Habitat

Creating a thriving habitat for monarch butteflies requires a thoughtful selection of plants that serve both as food sources and protective environments. Monarchs rely heavily on milkweed species for laying eggs and providing nourishment for their larvae.

In addition to milkweed, nectar-rich plants are essential for adult monarchs. These plants not only attract monarchs but also other pollinators, enhancing the overall biodiversity of the garden. Consider

incorporating native flowers such as coneflowers (Echinacea), asters, zinnias, and goldenrods is essential. These flowers bloom at different times throughout the season, ensuring a continuous food source for monarchs as they migrate. Photographers can capture stunning images of monarchs feeding on these vibrant blossoms, showcasing their beauty against a backdrop of colorful flora.

To support monarch populations, it's crucial to choose plants that are well adapted to the local climate and soil conditions. Native plants typically require less maintenance, making them an ideal choice for gardeners looking to create a sustainable habitat. Additionally, native plants are more resilient against pests and diseases, reducing the need for chemical interventions that could harm

monarchs and other beneficial insects. Photographers can document the natural interactions between monarchs and their native plant companions, highlighting the importance of ecological balance.

Creating a diverse plant community also helps to attract a wider variety of pollinators, which further benefits the ecosystem. By planting a mix of grasses, shrubs, and trees alongside nectar and host plants, gardeners can create a layered habitat that provides shelter and breeding grounds for monarchs and other wildlife. This diversity not only enriches the environment but also offers photographers a variety of settings and compositions to explore in their work. Capturing images of monarchs in different layers of the habitat can tell a compelling story about their ecological importance.

Lastly, understanding the migratory patterns of monarch butterflies can guide plant selection to ensure that gardens are attractive to monarchs during their migration. Planting species that bloom in late summer and early fall is particularly important, as these flowers provide essential sustenance for monarchs on their long journey to Mexico. Photographers can document this critical phase of the monarch's life cycle, capturing the butterflies as they prepare for migration. By creating a habitat rich in essential plants, photographers not only contribute to monarch conservation efforts but also gain unique opportunities to observe and photograph these remarkable butterflies in their natural environments.

Maintenance Tips for Butterfly Gardens

Creating a thriving butterfly garden requires ongoing attention to ensure it remains an inviting habitat for Monarch butterflies and other pollinators. Regular maintenance not only supports the health of the plants but also enhances opportunities for photographers seeking to capture these beautiful creatures in their natural environment. This subchapter outlines essential maintenance tips that will help sustain a butterfly-friendly garden.

First, regular watering is crucial, especially during dry spells. Monarch butterflies are attracted to healthy, vibrant plants, and ensuring that your garden remains well-hydrated is vital for plant growth. Use drip irrigation or a soaker hose to minimize water waste and provide consistent moisture directly to the roots. Additionally, consider mulching around plants to retain soil moisture and suppress weeds, which can compete for nutrients and space, potentially deterring butterflies from visiting your garden.

Pruning is another important aspect of maintenance. Deadheading, or removing spent flowers, encourages new growth and blooms, extending the blooming period of nectar-rich plants. This not only benefits the butterflies but also provides more opportunities for photographers to capture their interactions with the flowers. Regularly check for any dead, diseased, or overcrowded plants and prune them back to promote better air circulation and overall plant health, creating a more visually appealing garden.

Monarch butterflies are attracted to healthy, vibrant plants, and ensuring that your garden remains wellhydrated is vital for plant growth.

Pest management is essential for maintaining a healthy butterfly garden. While some insects are beneficial and attract butterflies, others can be harmful to the plants. Employ organic pest control methods,

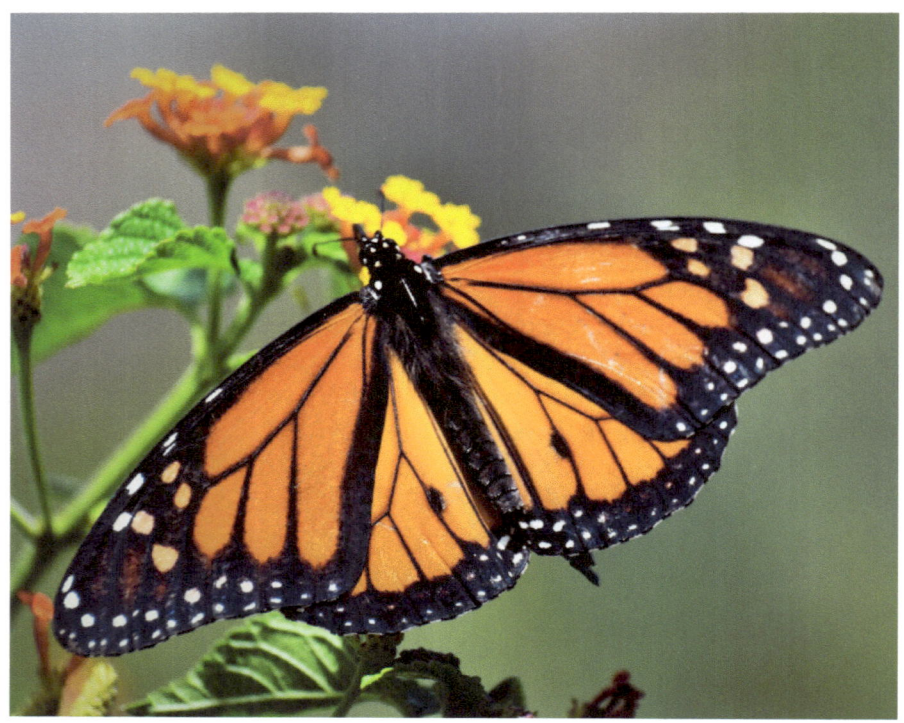

such as introducing beneficial insects like ladybugs or using insecticidal soap, to keep harmful pests at bay without threatening the butterfly population. This approach not only protects the plants but also preserves the garden as a suitable environment for Monarchs, allowing photographers to document the intricate relationships within the ecosystem.

Lastly, consider seasonal adaptations to your garden. As seasons change, so do the needs of the plants and the butterflies. In the fall, leave some plant stems standing to provide shelter for overwintering butterflies and other beneficial insects. In early spring, cut back dead foliage to make way for new growth while being careful to avoid disturbing any dormant caterpillars. These seasonal maintenance tasks not only support monarch butterfly conservation efforts but also enhance the aesthetic appeal of your garden, providing countless opportunities for stunning photography throughout the year.

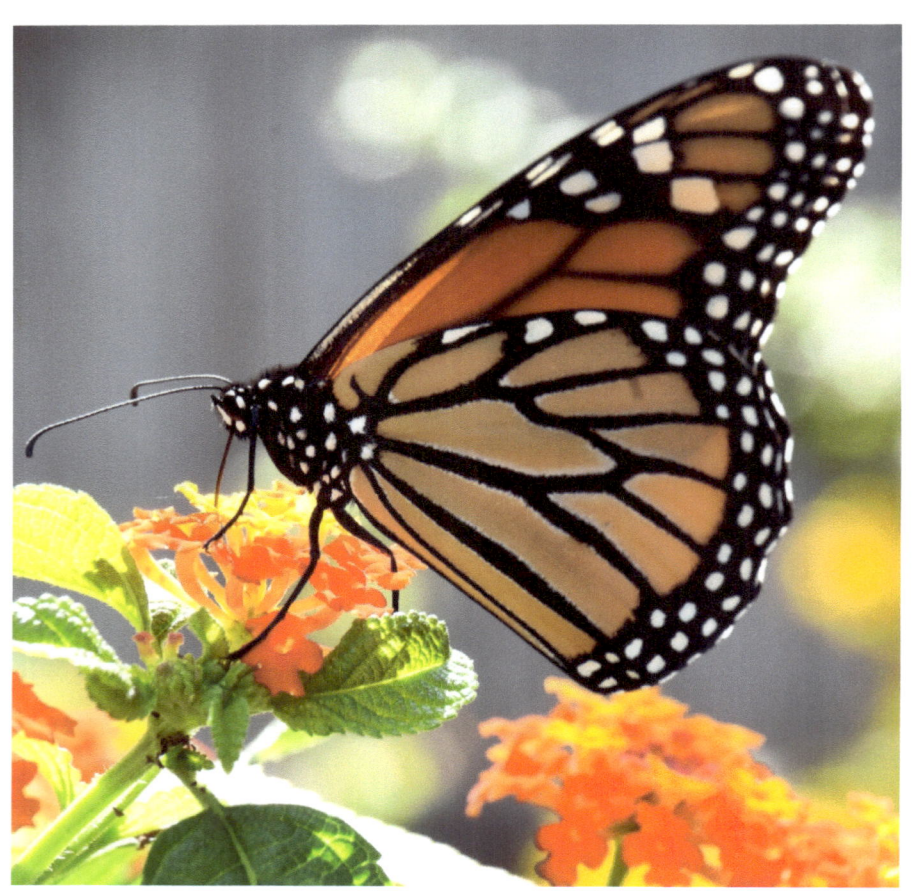

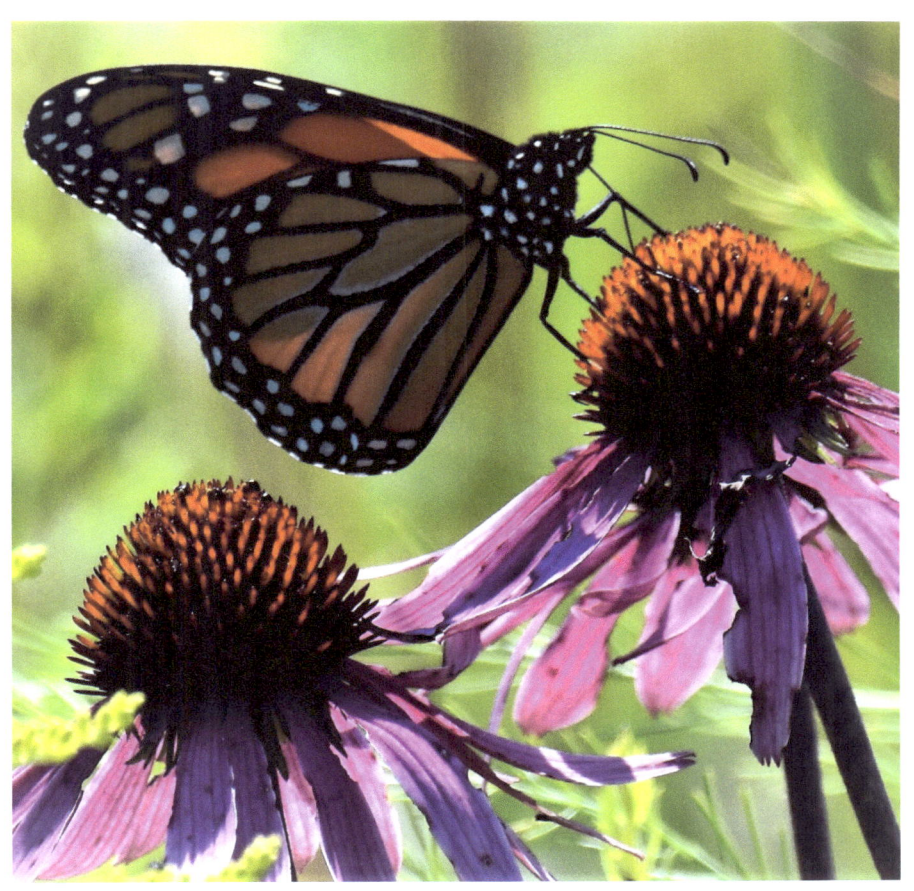

Chapter 7: Photo Techniques

Essential Equipment for Capturing Monarchs

Capturing the beauty of monarch butterflies requires more than just an eye for composition; it necessitates the right equipment to ensure that every detail is immortalized in your photography. Whether you are documenting their lifecycle, migration patterns, or the conservation efforts aimed at preserving their habitats, having the essential tools at your disposal can significantly enhance your ability to capture these magnificent creatures in their natural environment.

A quality camera is fundamental for any nature photographer. For photographing

 monarchs, a DSLR or mirrorless camera with interchangeable lenses is recommended. These cameras o☐er superior image quality, versatility, and control over exposure settings. A macro lens, typically in the range of 100mm to 180mm, is particularly advantageous for close-up shots, allowing you to capture the intricate details of the monarch's wings and antennae. Additionally, a telephoto lens can be bene☐cial for photographing monarchs from a distance, especially during migration when they may be more skittish.

Tripods and monopods are essential for stabilizing your camera, particularly in low-light conditions or for extended shooting sessions. A sturdy tripod can help reduce camera shake and is invaluable for long exposures or when photographing

 butterflies in low light or windy conditions. A monopod offers more mobility, allowing for quick adjustments while still providing some stability during handheld shooting. Investing in a good tripod or monopod can dramatically improve the quality of your images.

In addition to camera equipment, having the right accessories can enhance your photography experience. A circular polarizing filter is highly recommended to reduce glare and enhance the colors of the butterflies and their surroundings. This filter can help capture the vibrant hues of monarch wings against various backgrounds. A portable flash can also be useful for filling in shadows and illuminating subjects in darker environments, making the butterflies stand out more vividly.

Finally, understanding the habitats and behaviors of monarch butterflies is essential for successful photography. Equip yourself with field guides and resources on their migration patterns, life cycle, and preferred plants. Becoming familiar with the locations where monarchs are likely to be found, such as milkweed patches in gardens, increases your chances of capturing stunning images. By combining the right equipment with knowledge and patience, photographers can not only document the beauty of monarch butterflies but also contribute to conservation efforts by raising awareness through their photographic art.

Techniques for Photographing Monarchs in Flight

Techniques for photographing monarch butterflies in flight require a blend of

technical skill, patience, and an understanding of the butterfly's natural behavior. Capturing these delicate creatures in motion can be particularly challenging due to their quick movements and patterns, as well as the often unpredictable environmental conditions. To enhance your chances of success, familiarize yourself with the ideal times and locations for monarch sightings, which typically coincide with their migration periods in late summer and early fall. Knowing where monarchs are can significantly improve your photography and increase your productivity.

One of the best techniques for photographing monarchs on the move is to employ a fast shutter speed. Monarchs are known for their rapid wing beats, which can make it hard to capture a clear image if your settings are not

optimized. A shutter speed of 1/1000th of a second or faster is recommended to freeze their motion. Additionally, using continuous shooting mode allows you to take multiple frames in quick succession, increasing the likelihood of capturing a perfectly timed shot. This technique is particularly useful when combined with autofocus, which helps ensure that the monarch remains sharp in your photo.

Lighting plays a crucial role in wildlife photography, and capturing monarchs in ⬜ight is no exception. Early morning and late afternoon o⬜er the most favorable light conditions, as the golden hour provides a soft light that can enhance the vibrant colors of the monarch's wings. Position yourself accordingly to take advantage of this natural lighting to bounce light on to the monarch to

increase the detail in the photo. Additionally, using a lens with image stabilization can help counteract camera shake, especially when photographing at slower shutter speeds or from a distance.

Understanding the behaviors of monarchs can significantly improve your photographic results. Observing their movement paths and preferred perches can provide insights into when and where they are likely to take off or land. Monarchs are often seen gliding gracefully before a sudden burst of speed, so being patient and ready to capture these moments can yield stunning images. Furthermore, creating a monarch-friendly garden can attract these butterflies and provide excellent opportunities for special photography as they move from plant to plant, feeding on nectar.

Finally, the ethical considerations of photographing wildlife should not be overlooked. When photographing monarchs, strive to minimize your disturbance to their natural habitat. Avoid crowding them or disrupting their feeding areas, as this can cause stress and may impact conservation efforts. By respecting their environment and adhering to best practices in wildlife photography, you can not only enhance your skills but also contribute positively to the conservation of these remarkable insects. Balancing your passion for photography with a commitment to the well-being of monarchs will ensure that your work supports their continued presence in our ecosystems.

Tips for Macro Photography of Monarchs

Macro photography of monarch butterflies presents unique opportunities to capture

their beauty and intricacies while contributing to conservation awareness. When approaching this subject, it's essential to understand the behavior and habitat of these butterflies. Observing their patterns, especially during migration, can enhance your chances of fnding them in the right light and setting. Familiarize yourself with their preferred environments, such as milkweed patches, where they lay eggs and feed. Early mornings or late afternoons provide the best lighting conditions, allowing you to capture the delicate details of their wings while minimizing harsh shadows.

Investing in the right equipment is crucial for successful macro photography. A dedicated macro lens will allow you to get close to your subject without disturbing it. Ideally, a lens with a 100mm or greater focal

length will provide the detail needed to highlight the intricate patterns on a monarch's wings. Additionally, consider using a tripod or a monopod to stabilize your camera, especially in windy conditions. A reflector can help manage natural light and soften shadows, creating a unique image of your subject. Don't forget to bring along extra batteries and memory cards, as macro photography often requires patience and multiple shots to achieve the perfect composition.

Understanding monarch behavior can significantly enhance your photography. Monarchs are most active when the sun is shining, making midday an excellent time to capture them basking on flowers. However, remain patient and observant; monarchs often return to the same flowers. Use this to

your advantage by positioning yourself close to a favored nectar source and waiting for the butterfly to land. Capturing their unique life cycle stages—from caterpillars to chrysalises to adults—can also provide a compelling narrative in your photography portfolio, illustrating the beauty and fragility of their existence.

Incorporating the surrounding environment into your shots can add context and depth to your macro images. A well-composed photograph that includes milkweed plants or other native plants not only enhances the aesthetic but also tells a story about the monarch's habitat and its importance in the ecosystem. Experiment with di□erent anglesand perspectives; shooting from below or above can create unique compositions that highlight the monarch's interactions with its

environment. Using a shallow depth of focus will help isolate the monarch from the background, drawing attention to its vivid colors and intricate wing patterns.

Lastly, consider the broader implications of your macro photography. Each image you capture can serve as a powerful tool for advocacy and education regarding the monarch's conservation efforts. Sharing your photographs on social media and with local conservation groups can raise awareness about the challenges the monarch faces, including habitat loss and climate change. By combining your passion for photography with a commitment to conservation, you not only document the beauty of the monarch but also contribute to their survival and the health of the ecosystems they inhabit.

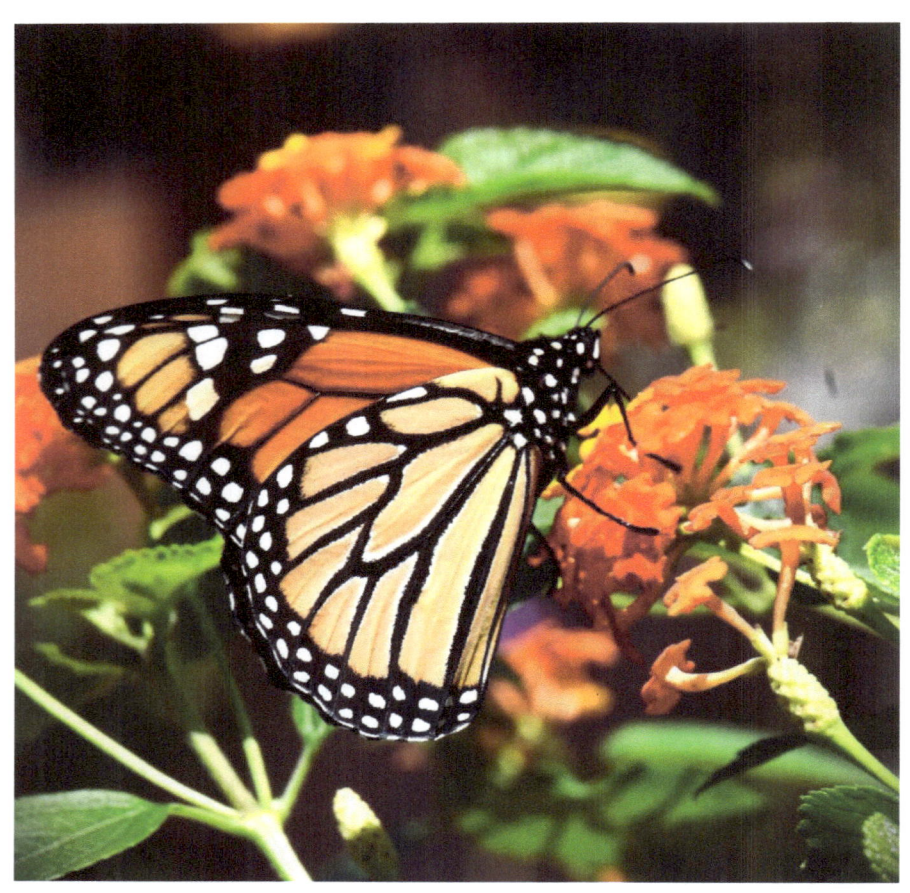

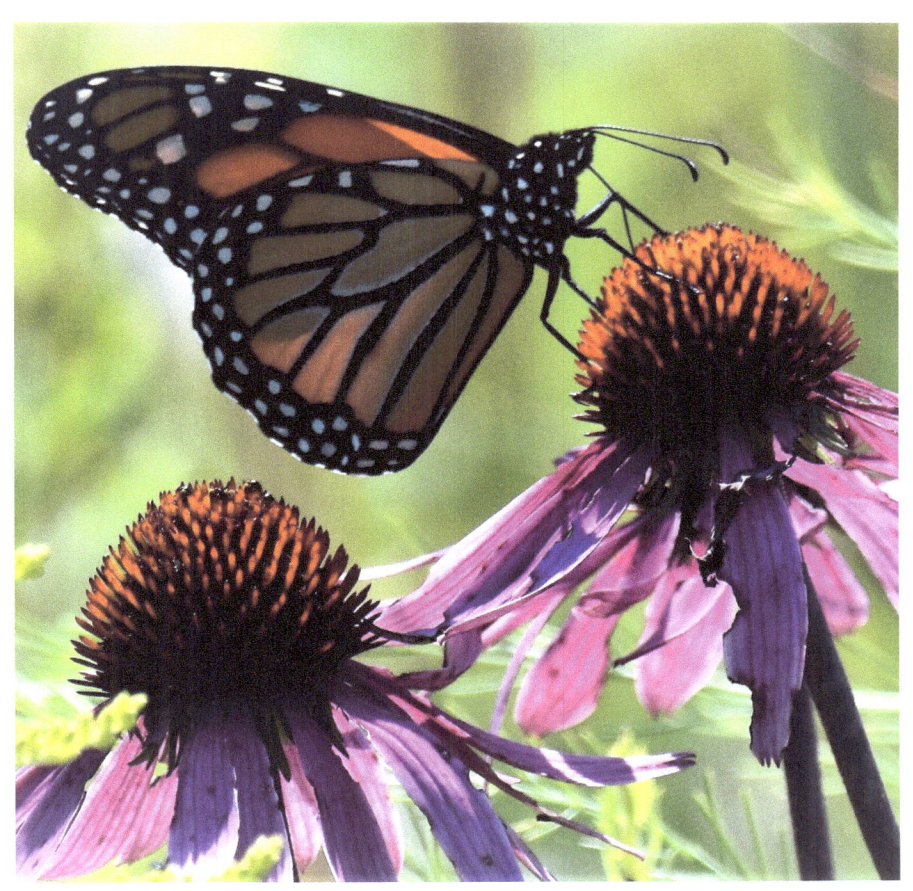

Chapter 8: Conclusion

The Future of Monarch

The future of monarchs is a significant concern, especially for photographers captivated by their beauty and the stories of their lives. Monarchs face threats from habitat loss, climate change, and pesticide use, endangering their migration and population. Photographers can play a vital role in highlighting these challenges, raising awareness, and inspiring conservation through their work. Understanding the factors affecting monarchs is essential for promoting their survival and ensuring future generations can appreciate their remarkable journeys.

One of the most pressing issues for monarchs is the degradation of their natural habitats. Urbanization and agricultural expansion have led to a dramatic loss of milkweed, the sole host plant for monarch caterpillars. Without this milkweed, the life cycle of the monarch is disrupted, impacting their ability to reproduce and thrive. Photographers can play a vital role in highlighting these changes through powerful imagery that illustrates both the beauty of milkweed and the stark realities of habitat destruction. By focusing their lenses on thriving milkweed patches and the monarchs that depend on them, photographers can evoke an emotional response that may motivate viewers to participate in conservation initiatives.

In addition to habitat loss, climate change poses a significant threat to monarch migration patterns. The monarch undertakes an incredible journey from Canada to Mexico, navigating thousands of miles across various landscapes. However, shifting weather patterns can disrupt their migration routes, and extreme weather events can destroy critical habitats. Photographers can document these migration patterns and environmental changes, capturing the essence of the monarch's journey while also raising awareness about the impact of climate change. By sharing these stories through visual narratives, photographers can educate their audience about the necessity of protecting the monarch's migratory corridors.

Gardening for monarch butterflies presents another avenue for conservation. Creating gardens with native plants, particularly milkweed and nectar sources, can significantly contribute to the survival of monarchs. Photographers have the opportunity to showcase these gardens, capturing the vibrant interactions between monarchs and their environment. By photographing the life cycle stages of monarchs in these gardens—from eggs to caterpillars to adults—photographers can provide valuable educational resources that encourage others to cultivate habitats conducive to monarch survival.

The impact of monarch butterflies on ecosystems cannot be overstated. As pollinators, they play a crucial role in maintaining the health of various plant species within their habitats. By documenting the interconnections between monarchs and their ecosystems, photographers can illustrate the broader implications of their conservation. Images that capture the delicate balance of nature, featuring monarchs alongside other wildlife, can serve as compelling reminders of the importance of biodiversity. Through their work, photographers have the power to inspire action and promote a deeper appreciation for the natural world, ultimately contributing to the enduring legacy of the monarch.

Engaging the Community in Conservation

Engaging the community in conservation efforts is crucial for the survival of the monarch and their habitats. As photographers, you possess a unique ability to document and share the beauty of these Engaging the community in conservation efforts is crucial for the survival of the monarch and their habitats. As

photographers, you possess a unique ability to document and share the beauty of these creatures, helping to foster a deeper appreciation for their role in our ecosystems. By collaborating with local organizations, schools, and environmental groups, you can amplify the message of conservation and inspire action within your community. The stories you capture through your lens can serve as powerful tools for advocacy, making it easier for others to understand the urgent need for protective measures.

One way is to engage the community is through educational workshops focused on the life cycle of the monarch. These sessions can be organized in collaboration with schools or community centers, where you can share your knowledge and photos to illustrate the various stages of development,

from egg to caterpillar to chrysalis and finally, the adult monarch. By visually demonstrating this transformative process, you can captivate the audience's attention and instill a sense of wonder about these insects. Such initiatives not only educate but also empower individuals to participate in conservation efforts, such as creating habitats that support the monarch lifecycle.

Creating gardens is another avenue for community engagement. Photographers can lead efforts to design and cultivate gardens that provide essential resources for monarchs, such as nectar-producing plants and milkweed, which are critical for caterpillar survival. By organizing community planting days, you can gather local residents, families, and fellow photographers to work together toward a common goal. Documenting these events through photography will enhance the visibility of your efforts and inspire others to participate, showcasing the beauty and importance of these gardens in supporting monarch populations.

In addition to hands-on initiatives, community engagement can also take place through social media platforms and local exhibitions. Sharing photographs of monarchs and their habitats can raise awareness about their migration patterns and the challenges they face. Hosting photography contests or exhibitions that focus on monarch conservation can encourage local artists to contribute their perspectives and experiences. This not only creates a sense of community involvement but also promotes a collective commitment to preserving these magnificent insects and their environments.

Finally, forming partnerships with conservation organizations can strengthen your efforts in engaging the community. Collaborating with groups dedicated to protecting monarch habitats allows you to tap into existing resources and networks. These partnerships can lead to joint campaigns that educate the public about the importance of conservation, provide training for aspiring butterfly photographers, and organize citizen science projects that track monarch populations. By working together, you can create a more significant impact, inspiring a community-wide movement toward the conservation of these vital species. pollinators and their ecosystems.

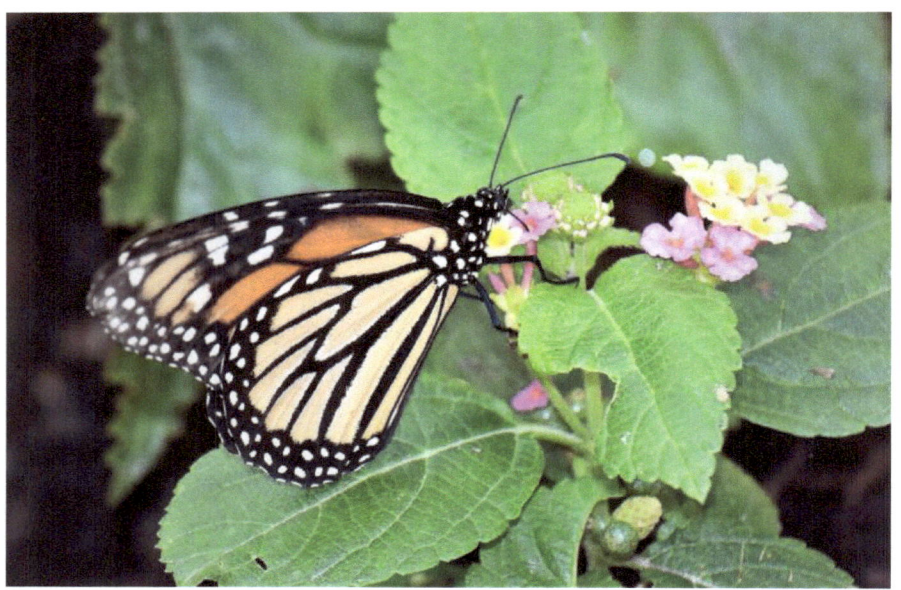

Final Thoughts for Photographers and Conservationists

As we conclude our exploration of the wondrous world of the monarch, it is essential to recognize the pivotal role that both photographers and conservationists play in the survival of these magnificent creatures. With their striking colors and delicate beauty, monarchs have become symbols not only of nature's artistry but also of the pressing need for environmental stewardship. By capturing their fleeting moments through the lens, photographers can raise awareness about the importance of conservation efforts and the significance of preserving habitats that support the entire life cycle of the monarch.

Understanding the migration patterns of monarchs is crucial for conservation. These insects embark on a remarkable journey each year, traveling thousands of miles between breeding and wintering grounds.

Photographers have a unique opportunity to document this migration, providing visual narratives that highlight the challenges faced by monarchs along their route. By sharing these stories, photographers can inspire others to engage in conservation efforts, whether that means planting native gardens to support larval food sources or advocating for the protection of critical habitats that monarchs rely upon during their journey.

In addition to documenting migration, photographers can play an instrumental role in educating the public about the monarch's life cycle. From egg to larva, pupa, and finally to adulthood, each stage presents unique opportunities for stunning photography. By

by capturing these stages, photographers can provide a deeper understanding of the species' biology and the environmental factors that impact their survival. This visual education fosters a greater appreciation for monarchs and encourages individuals to take action in their own backyards.

Gardening for monarch is another essential aspect of conservation that photographers can promote through their work. By showcasing native plants that attract and nourish monarchs, photographers can help foster a culture of gardening that prioritizes biodiversity. Educational content that emphasizes how certain plants support different life stages of monarchs can motivate individuals to transform their gardens into sanctuaries. This hands-on

approach to conservation not only benefits the monarch but also enhances the overall health of local ecosystems.

Ultimately, the collaborative efforts of photographers and conservationists can create a powerful force for change. Each photograph captures not only the beauty of the monarch but also serves as a call to action for preserving their habitats and migration routes. By working together, sharing knowledge, and inspiring others through the lens, both groups can contribute significantly to the conservation of monarchs and the ecosystems they inhabit. The future of these remarkable insects depends on our collective commitment to protecting their existence, ensuring that their wings of wonder continue to grace our skies for generations to come.

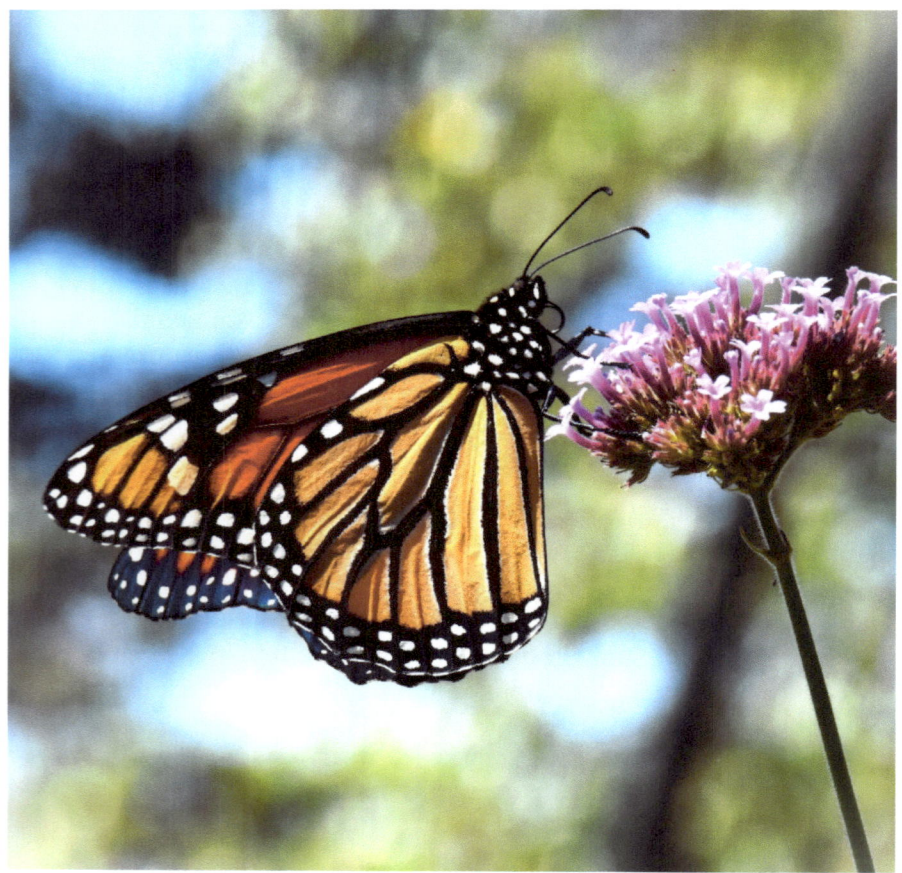

www.ingramcontent.com/pod-product-compliance
Lightning Source LLC
Chambersburg PA
CBHW040240220526
45473CB00001B/309